iMath
Readers

# Carnival Coins:
## How Will We Count Our Money?

**by Donna Loughran**

Content Consultant
David T. Hughes
*Mathematics Curriculum Specialist*

NORWOOD HOUSE PRESS
Chicago, IL

Norwood House Press
PO Box 316598
Chicago, IL 60631

For information regarding Norwood House Press, please visit our website at
www.norwoodhousepress.com or call 866-565-2900.


Special thanks to: Heidi Doyle
Production Management: Six Red Marbles
Editors: Linda Bullock and Kendra Muntz
Printed in Heshan City, Guangdong, China. 208N—012013

**Library of Congress Cataloging–in-Publication Data**

Loughran, Donna.

   Carnival coins: how will we count our money?/by Donna Loughran;
   consultant, David T. Hughes.
   p. cm.—(iMath)

   Includes bibliographical references and index.

   Summary: "The mathematical concepts of money, value, and counting dollars
   and cents are introduced as children attend a local carnival. Readers learn the
   differences between bills and coins, and are taught to skip count, count on, and
   compare values. This book includes a discovery activity, a history connection,
   and mathematical vocabulary introduction"—Provided by publisher.

Audience: 6–8
Audience: K to grade 3

ISBN 978-1-59953-552-4 (library edition: alk. paper)
ISBN 978-1-60357-521-8 (ebook)

1. Value—Juvenile literature.  2. Money—Juvenile literature.
3. Carnival—Juvenile literature. I. Title.

HG223.L68 2011
332.4—dc23
2012031019

# CONTENTS

**Note to Caregivers:**

Throughout this book, many questions are posed to the reader. Some are open-ended and ask what the reader thinks. Discuss these questions with your child and guide him or her in thinking through the possible answers and outcomes. There are also questions posed which have a specific answer. Encourage your child to read through the text to determine the correct answer. Most importantly, encourage answers grounded in reality while also allowing imaginations to soar. Information to help support you as you share the book with your child is provided in the back in the **Additional Notes** section.

**Bold** words are defined in the glossary in the back of the book.

4

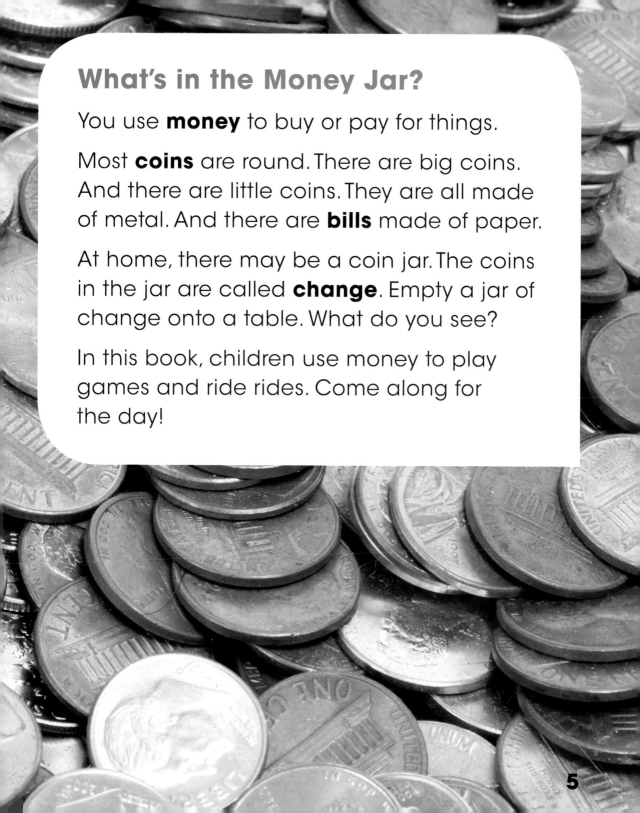

# What's in the Money Jar?

You use **money** to buy or pay for things.

Most **coins** are round. There are big coins. And there are little coins. They are all made of metal. And there are **bills** made of paper.

At home, there may be a coin jar. The coins in the jar are called **change**. Empty a jar of change onto a table. What do you see?

In this book, children use money to play games and ride rides. Come along for the day!

## How Much Money Is It?

Coins and bills are worth different amounts. Their **values** are given in **cents** (¢) and in **dollars** ($).

Look at the picture. It shows the front and back of some United States coins. Look from left to right. The first coin is a **penny**, or one cent (1¢). The second coin is a **nickel**, or five cents (5¢). The third coin is a **dime**, or ten cents (10¢). And the last coin is a **quarter**, or twenty-five cents (25¢).

This is the front of a penny, a nickel, a dime, and a quarter.

This is the back of a penny, a nickel, a dime, and a quarter.

How can you find how much a group of coins is worth?

**Idea 1: Count On with Skip Counting.** You can start at a number more than one. Then, you can count on by that number. This is called skip counting. You can use it to count money.

25¢     35¢     45¢     55¢

How much is this set of coins worth?

Start with the quarter and skip count by 10.

Do you think skip counting is a good way to count money? Why or why not?

**Idea 2: Count On with Ones.** You can count on with ones to count money.

5¢     6¢     7¢     8¢

How much is this set of coins worth?

Start with the nickel and count on with one.

Do you think counting on with ones is a good way to count money? Why or why not?

# Discover Activity

**Materials**
- coins
- empty jar

## A Handful of Money

Ask an adult to play with you.
Empty the coins from your piggy bank. Or
ask an adult to share some change that
you could play with.

Close your eyes. Grab some coins from the
pile. Count how much money you have in
your hand. Then, put the coins in a jar. Let
the adult take a turn.

Keep playing until all the coins are gone.
How much money did you count?

# Let's Count Our Money

The **carnival** [KAHR-nuh-vuhl] is in town! It opens tomorrow. It will have games and rides. There will be food and music, too.

Keisha and Jack meet at Rosa's house. The three friends want to go to the carnival. They must see how much money they have to spend.

"Do you know what this is?" Rosa asks.

"It's Pinky, your piggy bank," says Jack.

"Yes. And my money for the carnival is inside," Rosa says.

### 🔑 Did You Know?

Long ago, dish makers made bowls and jars from a clay called pygg [PIG]. People began to ask for "pygg jars" to hold their money. The dish makers shaped the jars into pigs. They put money slots on top of their clay "piggy banks."

Keisha holds up a glass jar. She says, "I brought my money, too." She shakes the glass. The money makes a clink-clink sound.

Jack holds up a paper bag. "Here's my money." He pats the bag. It makes a jingle-jingle sound.

"Let's put our money in three piles," says Rosa. "Then, we can count it."

Rosa's money is all coins. It makes a big pile. Keisha and Jack have coins and bills.

Rosa seems to have the most money. Why does it seem that way? Is her pile of coins larger? How can you find out how much money Rosa has?

Rosa counts her pennies. "Wow! I have 100 pennies. I know that 100 pennies equal $1."

"I have more coins," Rosa says. "I have 3 quarters, four dimes, and five nickels, too.
100¢ + 25¢ + 25¢ + 25¢ + 10¢ + 10¢ + 10¢ + 10¢ + 5¢ + 5¢ + 5¢ + 5¢ + 5¢."

"That's 100¢, 125¢, 150¢, 175¢, 185¢, 195¢, 205¢, 215¢, 220¢, 225¢, 230¢, 235¢, 240¢."

"I have 240¢ in all," says Rosa.

Jack says, "I have 2 one-dollar bills, ($2). And I have 2 quarters, 5 dimes, 2 nickels, and 7 pennies. That is:100¢ + 100¢ + 25¢ + 25¢ + 10¢ + 10¢ + 10¢ + 10¢ + 10¢ + 5¢ + 5¢ + 1¢ + 1¢ + 1¢ + 1¢ + 1¢ + 1¢ + 1¢."

How much money does Jack have in all?

Keisha says that she has the same amount of money as Jack. Who has more money? Is it Rosa? Or is it Jack and Keisha?

# Reading and Writing Money

Rosa's mother asks, "Do you need help?"

"We counted our money," says Rosa. "But how do we write the amounts?"

"Let me see," says Mrs. Gomez. "Rosa, you have 240¢. You can also write it as 240 cents."

"Jack, you have 317¢. You can also write it as 317 cents."

"Keisha also has 317¢. How much more money does she have than I have?" Rosa asks.

Mrs. Gomez says, "You can solve a **subtraction problem** to find the answer."

317¢ − 240¢

How much more money does Keisha have than Rosa?

# Connecting to History

"Where are coins made?" Rosa asks.

"At a **mint**," says Mrs. Gomez.

Keisha looks at a penny. "I wonder how a penny is made," she says.

"A machine punches circles out of a long strip of metal," Mrs. Gomez says. "The metal has a little bit of copper in it. Copper is what makes a penny look brown."

"The circles are called **blanks**. Workers heat the blanks to make the metal soft. Then, they put them in a washer. This makes them shine!"

Look for a tiny letter D or P on your coins. The coins with a D are made at a mint in Denver, Colorado. The coins with a P are made at a mint in Philadelphia, Pennsylvania.

"The shiny coins go in an **upsetting machine**. It puts a raised edge on the blanks."

"I didn't know machines could get upset!" says Jack.

Rosa laughs. She picks up a penny. "I can feel the edge."

"The blanks go into another machine. It presses pictures, numbers, and words into the soft metal."

"Wow! I didn't know it took so many steps to make a penny!" Rosa says.

# Math at Work

Many carnival workers use math. Some workers sell food. They take money and give change.

Some workers sell tickets to rides and games. They take money and wave to visitors, too.

There are workers at the rides. They have to measure to know how tall children are. That helps them be sure that children ride safely.

All of the workers at a carnival tell time. They know when to start work and when to finish.

These park workers wave to children who visit the park.

# At the Carnival

The carnival is exciting. The air smells of cotton candy and popcorn. There is organ music playing. And the games and rides are colorful.

"I want to get my face painted!" Rosa shouts.

"I want to ride the roller coaster!" Jack yells.

"I want to win a stuffed toy!" Keisha says, jumping up and down.

Mrs. Gomez says, "Check how much everything costs before you choose. "

"Let's meet back here in an hour."

The friends go to the roller coaster first. A ride costs 50¢.

Rosa takes some money from her pocket. She has 1 dollar, 4 dimes, and 5 nickels. What coins could she use to pay for the roller coaster ride?

"That was fun," Jack says. "Let's do it again!"

"Let's do some other things first," Keisha answers. "Let's play a game."

The friends walk to a big board. It has lots of balloons on it. A worker yells, "Hit a balloon with an arrow."

"Win a stuffed toy! Four arrows for only 175¢! Step up! Take your chances."

Keisha plays. She has 1 dollar ($1), 3 quarters, 3 nickels, and 2 pennies left. She uses her dollar. What coins does she give to the worker?

Pop! Pop! Pop! Pop! Keisha pops four balloons! She wins a huge stuffed tiger!

### ? What's the Word?

A carnival is like a fair. "The Animal Fair" is a song from the late 1800s. You can add different animals to write and sing a new song.

*I went to the animal fair,*

*The birds and the beasts were there,*

*The little raccoon by the light of the moon*

*Was combing his auburn hair.*

*The monkey bumped the skunk,*

*And landed on the elephant's trunk;*

*The elephant sneezed and fell to his knees,*

*And that was the end of the monk!*

*The monk! The monk! The monk!*

## Count Coins

Face painting is 125¢! Rosa has 1 dollar and 3 nickels left. How much more money does Rosa need?

"Rosa," says Jack. "Take this dime."

"Thanks, Jack," Rosa says. She buys a ticket.

Jack says, "I'll be right back. I'm going to buy a sucker."

One sucker costs 50 cents, plus 4 cents tax. Jack has 1 dollar ($1), 1 quarter, 4 dimes, 2 nickels, and 7 pennies left.

What coins could Jack use to pay for the sucker?

| 25¢ | 35¢ | 45¢ | 50¢ | 51¢ | 52¢ | 53¢ | 54¢ |

# iMath Ideas: The Last Ride

The friends want to go on one more ride. Each ride costs 50¢. They need 150¢ in all.

The children have 100¢, 2 dimes, 4 nickels, and 4 pennies in all. How can they find out how much they have in all?

**Idea 1: Count On with Skip Counting.** "We can start with the nickels and skip count by fives. 5¢, 10¢, 15¢, 20¢," Jack says. "Then, we can skip count by 10 to count the dimes. 30¢, 40¢."

**Idea 2: Count On with Ones.** "We can count on with ones for the pennies," Keisha says. "41¢, 42¢, 43¢, 44¢."

"Hmmm," Jack says. "We have one dollar and that's 100¢ and we just counted 44¢. So 100¢ plus 44¢ equals 144¢. Oh, no! We still need 6¢!"

"Here's 6¢," Mrs. Gomez says. The children yell thank you as they race away.

After the ride, Rosa says, "I had such a fun day counting coins! But, I had even more fun spending them!" Keisha and Jack agree.

# What Comes Next?

Ask an adult for help. Look at some food coupons together. Or, cut pictures out of newspapers that show food for sale. Then, follow these steps.

1. Get a large sheet of paper.

2. Draw a chart with two columns on the paper.

3. Paste or tape the pictures in the first column.

4. Draw coins next to each picture to show how much each food item costs.

Share your work with an adult. Ask the adult to add more pictures to your chart. Work together to show how much each thing costs.

# Glossary

**bills:** any paper money.

**blanks:** coins before pictures, numbers, or words are pressed into them.

**carnival:** a traveling show with games, rides, and special foods.

**cents:** money worth less than a dollar.

**change:** left over money or loose coins.

**coins:** money made out of metal.

**count on with ones:** to count on forward or backward by one. For example: 40¢, 41¢, 42¢, 43¢.

**count on with skip counting:** to count on forward or backward by a number larger than one. For example: 20¢, 25¢, 30¢, 35¢, 40¢.

**dime:** a ten-cent (10¢) coin.

**dollars:** paper pieces of money. For example, a one-dollar bill ($1) is the same as 100¢.

**mint:** a place where money is made.

**money:** dollars and cents.

**nickel:** a five-cent (5¢) coin.

**penny:** a one cent (1¢) coin.

**quarter:** a twenty-five (25¢) cent coin.

**subtraction problem:** to find a difference; to find what is left after one number is subtracted from another number. For example, 3 − 1 = 2.

**upsetting machine:** a machine that creates the raised edges of coins.

**values:** what things are worth.

# Further Reading

*FICTION*
**Counting on a Win,** by Marcie Aboff, Picture Window Books, 2009
**Walter Warthog's Wonderful Wagon,** by Barbara deRubertis, Kane Press, 2011

*NONFICTION*
**Lots and Lots of Coins,** by Margarette S. Reid, Dutton Juvenile, 2011
**Spending Money,** by Dana Meachen Rau, Gareth Stevens
Publishing, 2010

# Additional Notes

**The page references below provide answers to questions asked throughout the book. Questions whose answers will vary are not addressed.**

**Page 6:** You can count them.

**Page 10:** You can count the money to know who has the most.

**Page 11:** Jack has 317¢. Rosa has 240¢. Jack and Keisha have more money than Rosa.

**Page 12:** 317¢ − 240¢ = 77¢

**Page 16:** Rosa could pay with 4 dimes and 2 nickels, or 3 dimes and 4 nickels.

**Page 17:** One dollar is 100¢. Keisha needs 75¢ more. She could give the worker 1 dollar and three quarters. 100¢, 125¢, 150¢, 175¢

**Page 19:** Rosa has 100¢, 105¢, 110¢, 115¢ left. She needs 10¢ to get her face painted. Jack could use 1 quarter, 2 dimes, 1 nickel, and 4 pennies to pay for the sucker. 25¢, 35¢, 45¢, 50¢, 51¢, 52¢, 53¢, 54¢

# Index

# Content Consultant

**David T. Hughes**

David is an experienced mathematics teacher, writer, presenter, and adviser. He serves as a consultant for the Partnership for Assessment of Readiness for College and Careers. David has also worked as the Senior Program Coordinator for the Charles A. Dana Center at The University of Texas at Austin and was an editor and contributor for the *Mathematics Standards in the Classroom* series.